Good Character Traits

Adaptability

Ashley Lee

Explore other books at:
WWW.ENGAGEBOOKS.COM

VANCOUVER, B.C.

e WWW.ENGAGEBOOKS.COM

Adaptability: Good Character Traits
Lee, Ashley, 1995 –
Text © 2025 Engage Books
Design © 2025 Engage Books

Edited by: A.R. Roumanis
Design by: Mandy Christiansen

Text set in Myriad Pro Regular.
Chapter headings set in Anton.

FIRST EDITION / FIRST PRINTING

LIBRARY AND ARCHIVES CANADA CATALOGUING IN PUBLICATION

Title: Adaptability / Ashley Lee.
Names: Lee, Ashley, author.
Description: Series statement: Good Character Traits

ISBN 978-1-77878-735-5 (hardcover)
ISBN 978-1-77878-741-6 (softcover)

This project has been made possible in part by the Government of Canada.

Canada

Adaptability

Contents

What Is Adaptability?

Adaptability means being able to change when things around you change. Being adaptable helps people reach their **goals**.

Adapting often means changing the way you think about things. It is about finding new ways of doing things.

Why Is Adaptability Important?

The world is always changing. It is a normal part of life. Being adaptable helps people face new changes without getting too upset.

Adaptability also helps the world create new things. Scientists create new medicines when new illnesses show up.

What Does Adaptability Look Like?

Adaptable people stay calm when things change. They think about different ways to solve problems.

People who are adaptable do not give up easily. They try to think good thoughts and not get too upset.

Adaptable people may not like a change but they are able to be okay with it.

How Does Adaptability Affect You?

Being adaptable helps make you better at solving problems. This is because adaptable people try to solve problems instead of worrying about them.

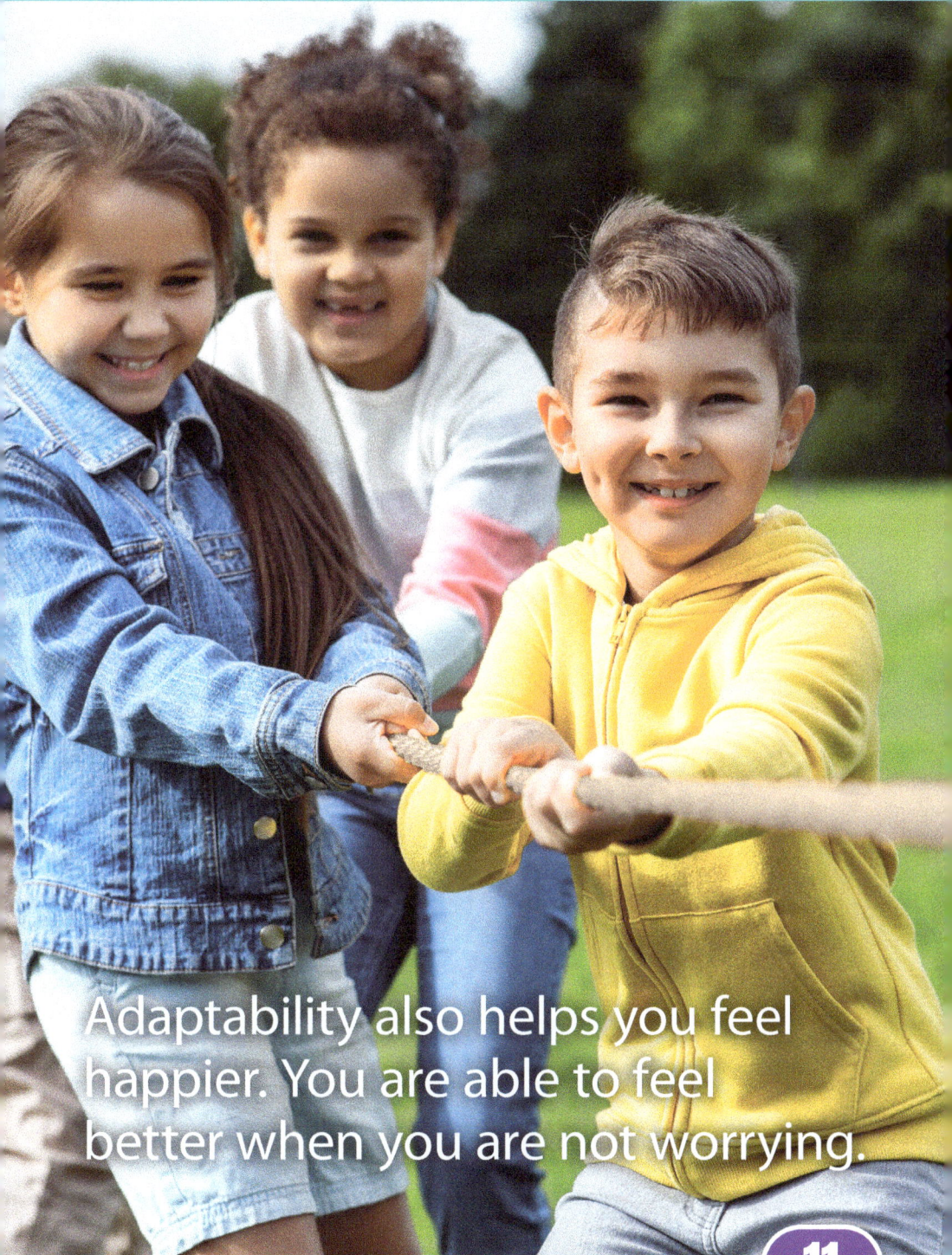

Adaptability also helps you feel happier. You are able to feel better when you are not worrying.

How Does Adaptability Affect Others?

Being adaptable can help other people stay calm when change happens. They will know everything is okay if you are not upset.

Being adaptable can also help you **support** other people. You are able to give more support to people who are not adaptable if you are not upset.

Key Word

Support: help or encourage someone.

Is Everyone Adaptable?

Not everyone is adaptable. Some people like **routines**, and that is okay.

Key Word

Routines: doing the same things at the same time each day.

Some people are only adaptable sometimes. But everyone can learn to be more adaptable with **practice**.

Key Word

Practice: do something over and over again to get better at it.

15

Is It Bad if You Are Not Adaptable?

It is not bad if you are not adaptable. But it is an important skill you should try to learn.

You may be unhappy more often if you are not adaptable. This is because the world is always changing.

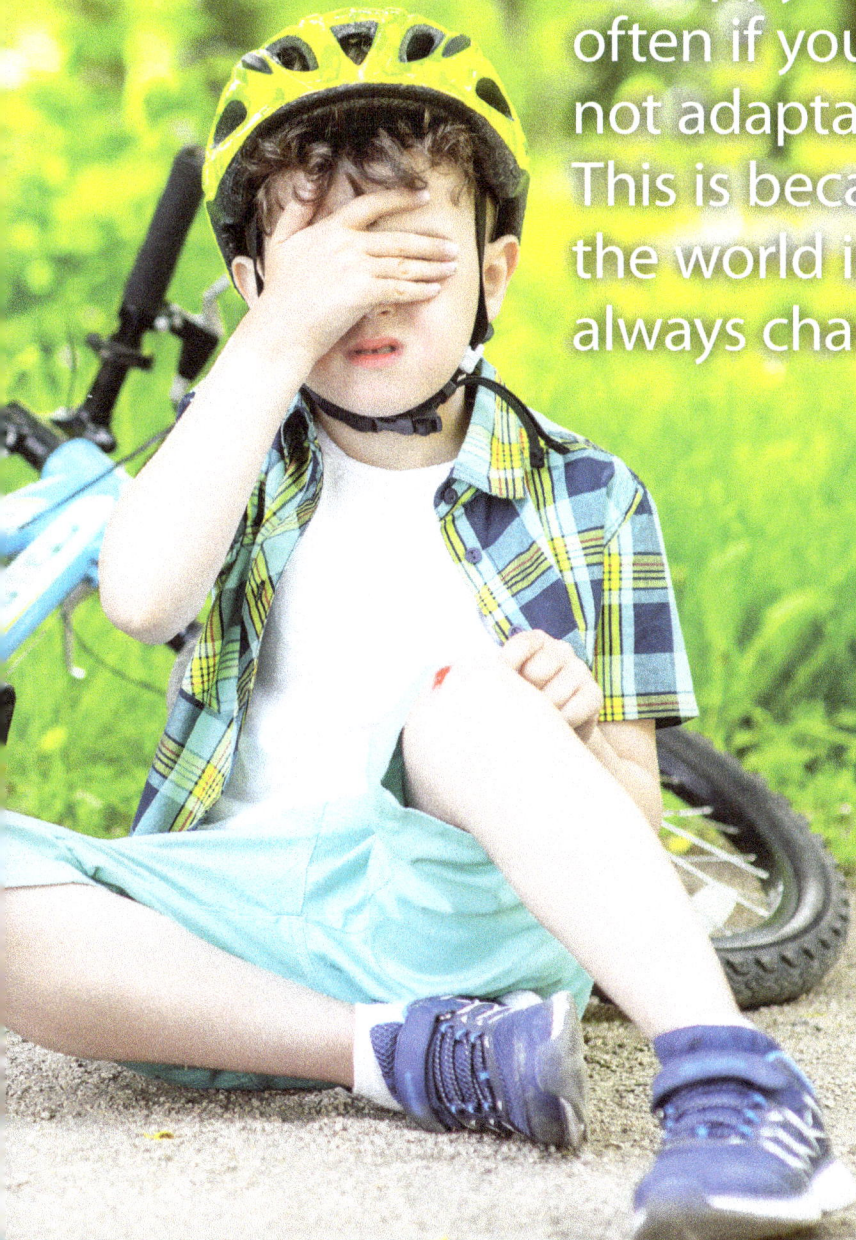

Does Adaptability Change Over Time?

Some people become more adaptable as they experience new things. They learn that not all change is bad. It can be good.

Some people with **mental health** problems may become less adaptable over time. They can often become more adaptable again if they get help.

Key Word

Mental health: the health of your mind.

Is It Hard to Be Adaptable?

Adapting is hard for some people. Change can make them feel worried or fearful because they do not know what will happen.

Adapting can be hard when you are young because you are learning about so many new things.

Some people find it easy to adapt to new things. The idea of something new and different may make them excited.

How Can You Learn to Be More Adaptable?

Try not to see change as a bad thing. Think of all the ways a change may be good for you.

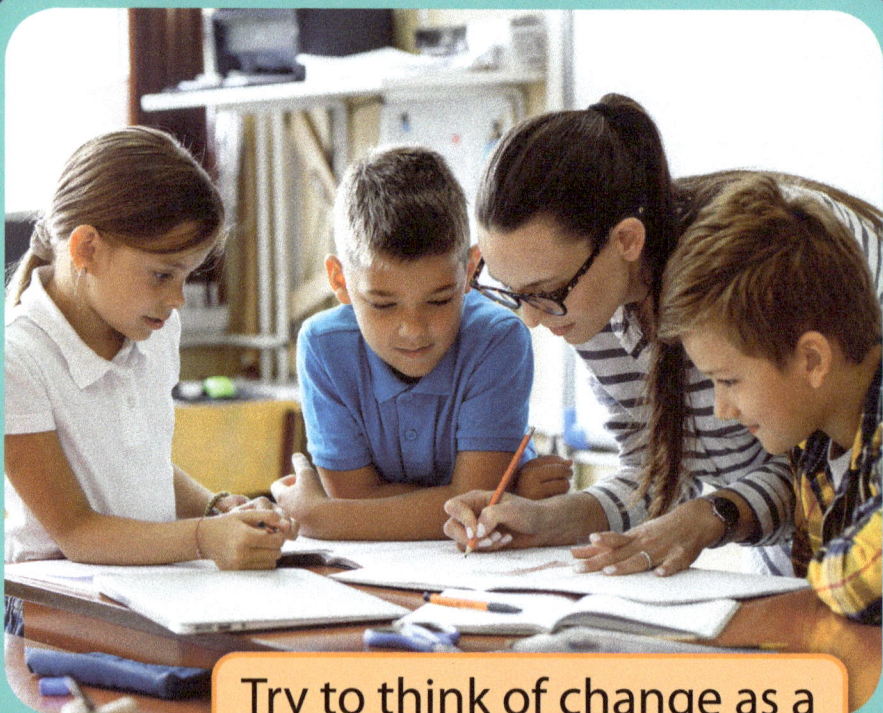

Try to think of change as a chance to learn and grow.

Try new things even if they seem scary. This will help you feel good about yourself and your **abilities**.

Key Word

Abilities: power to do things.

How Can You Help Others Be More Adaptable?

Be kind and **patient** when you see others having a hard time with change. Adapting is harder when other people push you to do it.

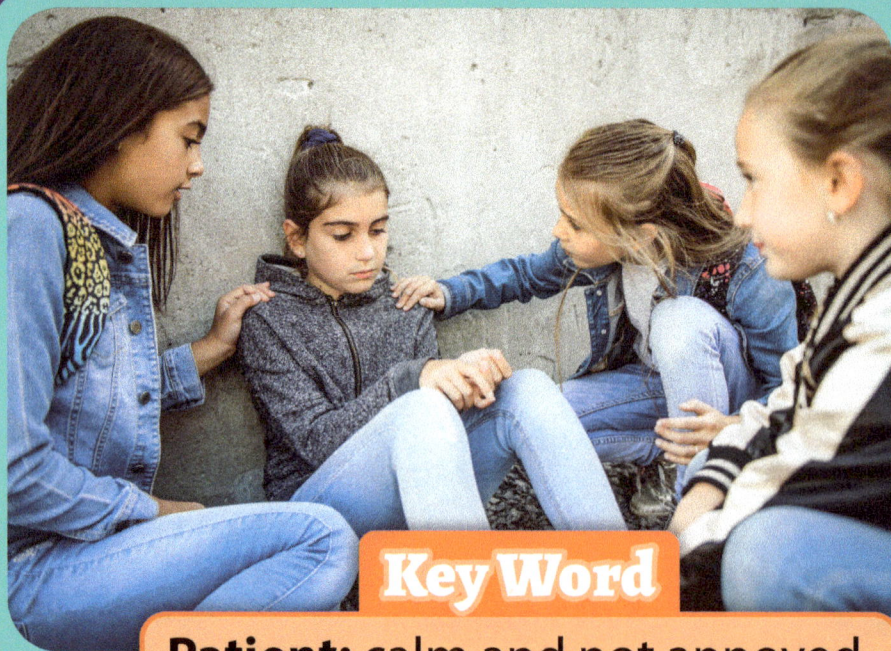

Point out the ways change can help someone learn. Talk about all the ways change can be a good thing.

How to Be Adaptable Every Day

1. Try to learn from your mistakes.

2. Look for the good parts of every change.

3. Be open to new ideas.

4. Ask for help when you need it.

Adaptability Around the World

People burn **fossil fuels** to make energy. But burning fossil fuels is harming the planet.

Key Word

Fossil fuels: energy sources that cannot be renewed.

People are finding new ways to make energy that do not harm the planet. Adapting is helping them save Earth.

Quiz

Test your knowledge of adaptability by answering the following questions. The questions are based on what you have read in this book. The answers are listed on the bottom of the next page.

2 What does adaptability help the world create?

1 Is adapting about finding new ways of doing things?

3 Does being adaptable help make you better at solving problems?

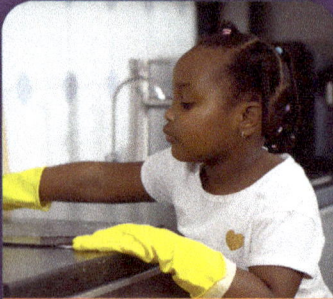

5 Is all change bad?

4 Can everyone learn to be adaptable?

6 What should you do when you see others having a hard time with change?

Explore Other Level 2 Readers.

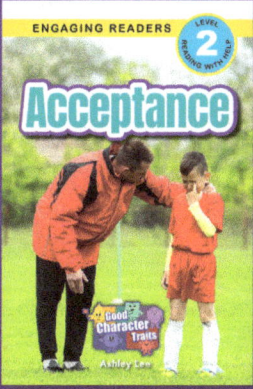

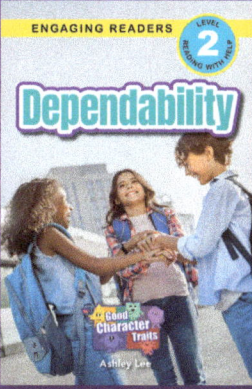

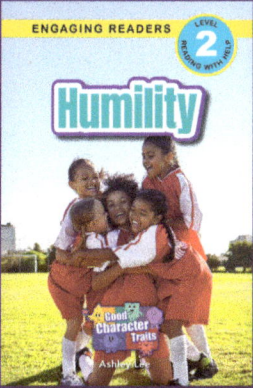

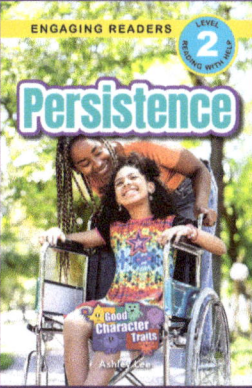

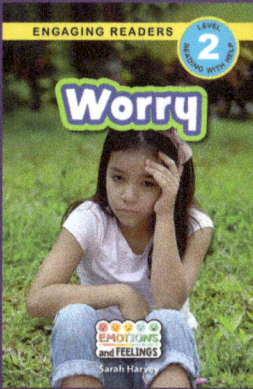

Acceptance

Dependability

Forgiveness

Humility

Persistence

Gratitude

Grief

Love

Worry

Visit www.engagebooks.com/readers

www.ingramcontent.com/pod-product-compliance
Lightning Source LLC
Chambersburg PA
CBHW052034030426
42337CB00027B/5009